for Claire and Jim
with affection
and in celebration of
their 25th Anniversary —

Bev

GEORGIA O'KEEFFE

Beverly Gherman
July · 1986

Georgia with skull painting, 1931.   The Bettmann Archive

GEORGIA

The "Wideness and

O'KEEFFE

Wonder" of Her World

by Beverly Gherman

ATHENEUM NEW YORK 1986

Library of Congress Cataloging-in-Publication Data

Gherman, Beverly.
  Georgia O'Keeffe : the wideness and wonder of her world

  Bibliography: p. 125.
  Includes index.
  SUMMARY: A biography of a foremost American artist,
beginning with her early fascination with color
and light, the struggle for recognition in a man's field,
her relationship with Alfred Stieglitz, and the final
glory of her New Mexico years.
    1. O'Keeffe, Georgia, 1887-1986—Juvenile
literature.   2. Painters—United States—Biography—
Juvenile literature. [1. O'Keeffe, Georgia, 1887-1986.]
2. Artists]   I. Title.
ND237.O5G4   1986   759.13 [B] [92]   85-26860
ISBN 0-689-31164-8

Published simultaneously in Canada by
Collier Macmillan Canada, Inc.
Composition by P & M Typesetters, Waterbury, Connecticut
Printed and bound by Fairfield Graphics, Fairfield, Pennsylvania
Designed by Mary Ahern
First edition

To my family and friends who have shared this experience with me for a very long time, and especially to Robbie, who has traveled in my heart every step of the way.

CONTENTS

ACKNOWLEDGMENTS

My gratitude to the many individuals at museums, libraries, newspapers, and archives throughout the country who gave me much more than their time.

Special thanks to Janet, who introduced me to Georgia O'Keeffe's world; to O'Keeffe herself,whose art would not let me rest; to Laurie Lisle for writing her book about O'Keeffe and allowing me to use many of its personal details; to Sue Davidson Lowe for her book about her great-uncle, Alfred Stieglitz, and her kindness in arranging for me to include a photograph by Josephine B. Marks from that book; and to Mary Kay Karzas and Chatham Hall for permission to use Georgia's early drawings.

In creating this book of my own I owe a great deal to the generosity of friends: Marilyn Sachs gave me her expertise and constant encouragement. Maxine Schur never let me stop revising. Jeanie Kortum-Stermer wove all the threads together. Debra and Ron were never too busy to listen to the latest version. My editor, Marcia Marshall, promptly answered every question and met every need. Cindy served as my local critic, Greg as my long distance critic, while Chuck was always my enthusiastic supporter.

AUTHOR'S NOTE

When I read Georgia O'Keeffe's book about her paintings,
I was overwhelmed by the power of her forthright words
as she described her work. I studied every painting,
poster, and photograph I could find. I read Laurie
Lisle's book, *Portrait of an Artist*. I haunted the
library to find other articles and information. I even
made a visit to New Mexico. I wanted to know as much
as possible about Georgia O'Keeffe because she had lived
her life in a special way, at a time when it was not
easy for women to do so. She became an artist when
others expected her to become a teacher. She didn't
paint the pictures others expected her to; she painted
canvases that expressed her fresh view of the world.
She had to be strong and sure and separate from others.
I wanted to tell these things about her, and more. . . .

GEORGIA O'KEEFFE

. . . All I know is that one
understands only what one loves.

Marc Chagall, 1978

The Brightness

GEORGIA O'KEEFFE recently celebrated her ninety-seventh birthday in her adobe home overlooking the rolling hills of New Mexico. Over the years her face has become as etched and as famous as her paintings of those red hills.

Georgia's uncanny appreciation for her surroundings began in infancy. She insisted she could remember her very first outing, when she was carried from the hazy rooms of the family's farmhouse into sunlight. Propped against large pillows on a familiar red and black quilt, her eyes filled with a blueness that seemed to stretch forever over her head. She was dazzled by the brilliance of the sun. It warmed her face and arms. It skipped along the stars and flowers of the quilt and glistened against the prickly grass beyond her.

Georgia noticed her mother's friend Winnie, whose long dress was dotted with dainty blue flowers and gathered together into a puffy bustle. She was startled by Winnie's mass of curly blond hair after having seen only the straight, dark hair of her mother and aunts.

Most vivid of all to Georgia, then scarcely a year old, was the brightness of that day. It forced her to squint at the white farmhouse glaring against the dark, curving drive. It collided with the high hedge and formed shadows that crawled along the path before her.

Years later, when Georgia related her earliest memory, her mother kept insisting it was impossible to remember things that happened before you could walk or talk. But Georgia was adamant and described the scene in such sharp detail that her unbelieving mother finally had to admit Georgia's memory was not only accurate, but quite amazing.

Georgia's fascination with her environment grew along with her. From the settings in which she lived she chose the subjects for her paintings: the weathered barns of the lush Wisconsin farm lands, the canyons of the Texas plains, and the towering skyscrapers of urban New York.

Before she began to paint she studied every detail of a scene. Into her oil paints she mixed her feelings about what she saw and then added a good portion of her vivid imagination. By the time she completed a canvas it was not at all a reproduction of the original setting. Instead Georgia had simplified everything to create the essence of what she saw. Her barns seem strangely held in place by heaps of grain. Her city trees are lit by the eerie effect of moonlight, her skyscrapers are magical columns defying gravity.

When Georgia was in her early thirties, she decided to devote her life to working as an artist. Until then she could paint only in free moments away from teaching.

She had moved to New York City, where every day she watched crowds of busy people rush through their lives without taking a moment to look at anything beautiful. Georgia chose to paint enormous flowers that would make everyone stop and notice. She wanted others to feel what she felt when she held a flower, studied its parts, breathed its fragrance, and saw in it a whole "world for the moment."

It had long been the custom for artists to paint flowers with small, delicate brush strokes. Georgia broke the rules. She filled her brush with rich, thick paint and spread the petals of a morning glory to the very edge of a three or four foot canvas. She pene-

Poppies, 1950. Oil on canvas, 36 x 30". Milwaukee Art
Museum Collection, Gift of Mrs. Harry Lynde Bradley

trated into the inner layers of the iris. Sometimes she magnified the heart within an open white rose, an orchid, a brilliant red poppy until its center became the whole canvas.

These were powerful paintings which made people notice. Some said they felt transformed into tiny insects peering into Georgia's exaggerated blossoms. The other painters—mostly men who exhibited along with her—were uneasy with her bold use of color. But most viewers and critics who wrote about her work echoed her mother's earlier thought that Georgia was out-of-the-ordinary in the way she looked at the world.

Georgia's paintings of enormous flowers, canvases celebrating the skies, and floating animal skulls are her interpretations of nature. They vibrate with an unusual strength while at the same time they force us to ask questions. Why is the skull drifting peacefully above the hills? Is the abstract shape we see really the center of a flower? Do canyons truly overflow like volcanic outpourings? What is Georgia O'Keeffe trying to tell us? What in her life made her depict our world in this way?

2

Beneath the Branches

I N THE MID-1800s Georgia O'Keeffe's grandparents joined other European immigrants who traveled across the United States to settle in the fertile Wisconsin plains. They began by clearing the forests, building simple, sturdy homes and barns, and then planting crops of wheat, corn, and sorghum. Before long, the air was fragrant with newly turned earth and sweet grasses.

Georgia's grandparents settled on adjoining farms in southern Wisconsin, near the small village of Sun Prairie. Her father, Francis, was a young boy when his own father died. He quit school to help his mother and brothers run their thriving farm. Francis loved working the land and always managed to keep a smile on his face, and later, a treat in his pocket for his children.

Georgia's mother, Ida, lived on the neighboring farm until her father gave up the hard work of farming and returned to his native Hungary. Her mother took the family to live in the nearby university town of Madison. Ida, then sixteen, was a serious young woman who loved literature, music, and art.

When Francis persuaded Ida to marry him in 1884, she gave up city life and returned to the prospering O'Keeffe farm, which by then had grown to more than three hundred acres. The following year, Francis and Ida had their first child, a son, whom they named Francis, Junior. Georgia was born almost two years later, and by the time she was twelve, she had four sisters and two brothers.

In those years the O'Keeffe farmhouse was filled with the bustling activity of children; Aunt Jenny, who came to help Ida; other visiting relatives; farmhands; and often the local schoolteacher, who boarded with the family.

It had been a more subdued time when Georgia was born in her parents' bedroom in the blustery November of 1887. She spent the first months of life in shadowy rooms lit by flickering kerosene lamps and heated by wood-burning stoves. Throughout the icy winter, the rolling plains around the farmhouse lay hidden beneath a heavy gray coverlet. Gradually, the sun's rays transformed the land into a vibrant patchwork of crops, wildflowers, and blossoming trees, all of which would become Georgia's indelible memory of the spring world.

The following summer, eighteen-month-old Georgia scampered onto the dusty drive leading to the house, unaware that she could be harmed by an oncoming horse and buggy. She wanted to touch the whirling particles of dust she had seen. She wanted to sit right in the hot earth, sift it through her fingers, let it fly in the air, and even feel its grittiness in her mouth. In later years she would have the same urge to taste her oil paints as she squeezed them from fresh tubes onto her clean glass palette.

Once she began to talk, Georgia never stopped asking questions about the world. She wondered, "If Lake Monona rose up, way up, and spilled all over, how many people would be drowned?" or "When two big clouds bump together, is *that* thunder?"

Six-year-old Georgia was fascinated by the shells Grandmother O'Keeffe kept on whatnot shelves in the parlor. She would sneak into the room, carefully select a clam shell, and hold it tightly against her ear to hear its message from the sea. Afterward, with her finger she would trace its cool, intricate lines. For her the shell was a complete world of its own. She would grow up admiring the simplicity and beauty of each sea shell she collected.

If sea shells provided Georgia a miniature view of nature, the farm offered her nature on a grand scale. In the fall before she was eight, Georgia walked with her father through the fields to check the height of the growing corn against her shoulders. She had been measuring it since the seedlings first poked through the rich chocolate earth; and that year, she would see the newly invented harvester pluck off ripe ears and cut down the mature corn stalks. After the harvest, she knew that Francis and his helpers would begin all over again to turn the fields and prepare them for spring planting.

Georgia's life revolved around the growing seasons on the farm. She looked forward to tramping through the crusty snow of winter or wading in the creek during the hottest days of summer. In between, she could hardly wait for the days of early spring, when she would see the whole land become a powder puff of bursting buds.

Georgia also studied herself. What she found in the glass was a plain, thin face with enormous blue eyes and thick brown hair. Yet people often told her how much she resembled her father and, since she found him a handsome man, she felt proud and secretly hoped she was handsome, too. She was certainly definite about how she liked to appear. If her sisters were going to wear their hair braided one day, she insisted that her dark hair be left straight; if they donned white stockings, hers had to be another color. She thought she looked better without bows or ribbons and tried to tell her sisters they should not wear such frills either.

While Georgia shared her father's looks and love of nature, she grew to appreciate her mother's feelings for the arts. Ida passed on her love of books to her children by reading to them every evening. Seated on the plush sofa, she gathered them to hear the next chapter of *The Deerslayer*. In her mind, nine-year-old Georgia glided in the canoe and climbed the Eastern peaks beside Deerslayer, his friend Hurry Harry, and the Indian chief, Chingachgook.

Ida's warm, expressive voice also produced vivid pictures of rugged pioneer life as she read adventure stories about the Wild West exploits of Kit Carson, or Billy the Kid. Georgia would be lured to Texas and the Southwest to experience their rugged beauty for herself as soon as she could.

Georgia's greatest pleasure of all was to be solitary. When her brothers and sisters gathered to play tag inside the damp, cool dairy, Georgia would steal off by herself to her private place beneath the branches of the gnarled hemlock and apple trees. There she would kneel to unpack and arrange each member of her miniature china doll family.

She had sawed slits in two thin boards and joined them to make the walls of a house, which she stood in thick grass. The tall weeds served as forests, gravel shaped its walkways, and a filled dishpan formed its nearby lake. With patient hands, Georgia stitched the clothes for her dolls and constructed their furniture. Her apron pockets were always filled with fabric remnants she had found in the sewing basket.

Sunlight became her silent companion. She saw it dance through the leaves, flickering and blinking while she remained under the trees for hours, never feeling lonely. "If only people were trees, I might like them better," she was to say when she was older.

3

Crazy Notions

THE O'KEEFFE CHILDREN studied at the same one-room schoolhouse their parents had attended on the edge of the farm. Ida found a neighbor to give art lessons to her three oldest daughters because the school did not offer such classes.

At first Georgia paid little attention to the lessons. She was too busy with her doll family. Once she had tried to draw a man who was bending over at the middle, something her dolls could not do. She kept wetting her black lead pencil to make darker lines on the brown paper bag, but hard as she tried, her man wouldn't bend his knees correctly. Ready to give up, she discovered that her man looked just fine if she turned the paper around. Then he was a man lying on his back with legs straight up!

14

During lessons, Georgia learned to draw cubes and other shapes from a guide book, and she copied pictures that looked pleasing to her. But one day she discovered a special picture in one of her mother's books. It was a tiny pen and ink drawing called *Maid of Athens*. Georgia was so moved by the beauty she found in its simple lines that it made her want to create beautiful drawings of her own.

When her mother next found a real painter to teach Georgia and her sisters, Georgia began to take the lessons more seriously. Every Saturday the sisters traveled by horse and buggy to the nearby village of Sun Prairie, where Mrs. Sara Mann taught them the difficult watercolor technique of applying colored paints to dampened paper. They continued to practice by making copies from pictures Mrs. Mann kept stored in a large cupboard.

Once Georgia painted a bouquet of lush red roses and another time she copied handsome race horses. If the results were not quite right, Mrs. Mann made corrections directly on the girls' pictures. It annoyed Georgia to see Mrs. Mann's brush strokes whenever she looked at her work, and she was very glad when those watercolors were lost.

At twelve, Georgia moved into a tower room of her own, which her father had built for her at the top of the spacious farmhouse. By then she had been

Georgia's birthplace as it appeared many years later. From
her tower room, she found challenging scenes to paint.
State Historical Society of Wisconsin

taking art lessons for almost two years and thought her drawings looked as good as the originals from which she copied. But she was tired of merely copying from static pictures. She wanted the challenge of painting actual scenes.

Through her tower windows, she could see moonlight glowing on the snow. It was important to her to find the right color to make the snow look bright and glistening against the dark trees. After many unsuccessful attempts, she found the perfect solution. If she left the paper white, added dark blue to the nearby oak tree, and lavender-gray to the evening sky, she could capture the scene.

Next she tried to depict a lighthouse at the edge of the sea with palm trees along the horizon—things she had seen only in a geography book. Her goal was to make the sun shine against the bright sky. Every time she added color to the yellow sun, it turned muddier. Then she realized that if she used a cloudy sky for the setting, the sun would seem to glow.

The more work she did on her own, the more confident she felt. She would become an artist, she announced to a young friend, Lena. Georgia could not say what kind of artist she would be, nor had she read about other women who had become artists, but she felt sure of her decision. She didn't worry that some in the family thought it was another of her "crazy notions." She just knew that she was haunted by the tiny *Maid of Athens* drawing, which she had found so beautiful.

In 1901, when Georgia was almost fourteen, her mother decided she should leave home to attend Sacred Heart Academy, near the town of Madison. Ida recognized Georgia's developing talent and wanted to provide her with special training so that she could become an accomplished art teacher. It probably never occurred to Ida that Georgia would do more than that. In the early 1900s women could certainly teach, even if they could not yet vote or hold office or obtain higher education at many universities.

Sister Angelique was the art instructor at Sacred Heart. On the first day she asked the students to copy a white plaster cast of a baby's hand. Georgia took a stick of charcoal and began drawing an outline of the hand. She pressed more and more firmly as she filled in her lines, crushing the charcoal into ash all over her paper, her hands, and her smock. She continued working until she completed a small, heavy picture, which was very similar in style to her earlier upside-down man.

Pleased, she took it to Sister, who opened her eyes wide and twisted her mouth angrily as she stared at the drawing. She scolded Georgia for making such a cramped, messy picture.

Taking a fresh piece of charcoal, Sister Angelique made large, sweeping lines to illustrate what she expected. Georgia stood there humiliated, fighting back tears, her face flushing to a deep, hot crimson. To herself she vowed never again to draw so small. She would always make her pictures larger and lighter than they should be.

By the end of the school year, the art room was hung from one end to the other with Georgia's light, airy paintings. On each drawing Sister had written "G. O'Keeffe" with very dark pencil. From the back of the room, Georgia noticed with dismay that her name stood out more distinctly than her drawings. Perhaps this moment remained in her mind and influenced Georgia to leave her future paintings unsigned. Her paintings would have to identify themselves.

4

From Wisconsin to Williamsburg

D URING THE YEARS Georgia was growing up, her father continued to purchase and develop land adjoining the O'Keeffe farm until he owned nearly six hundred acres. He also bought and sold cattle, ran a successful dairy, and continued to supervise the planting and harvesting of numerous crops. It was a rigorous life for Francis O'Keeffe.

When the last of his three brothers died from tuberculosis in 1898, Francis became very fearful about his own health. He worried that he might be next in line to come down with the disease. An extremely harsh winter added another concern. The temperature dropped more than thirty degrees below zero, freezing the well water and all the food stored in the cellar. It was too much. Francis decided to sell the farm and take Ida and the children to the warmer and healthier climate he had heard about in Williamsburg, Virginia.

While the family was resettling, Georgia went to live with her Aunt Lola in Madison. She found life in the city quite a change from the rural setting she had always known, with its friendly one-room schoolhouse and broad outdoor spaces. Even the previous year at the convent school was hardly preparation for so many new sights and sounds.

The town of Madison, only twenty miles from Sun Prairie, was a bustling community of several thousand people. It was possible to travel across town on the latest automated trolleys, to watch new homes springing up, and notice how quickly new businesses were becoming established.

Aunt Lola's house was on a street lined with other small, tidy homes, their neat yards a contrast to Sun Prairie's expanse of grazing land and patches of colorful crops. From her upstairs room Georgia could at least view distant hills beyond the lapping waves of Lake Monona, but she no longer worried that the water might rise and drown them all.

Georgia began to measure the seasons by activities in town rather than by growing crops and work schedules on the farm. During the winter she saw that Madison had outdoor skating on the lake and a sledding hill so steep that you could swoop down it and then fly up an adjoining hill without stopping. In summer there were rowboats for crossing the lake to explore Indian villiages on the other side.

Georgia was enrolled at Madison High School, a sturdy building in which nine hundred students moved from room to room for classes, jostling and greeting one another. There were enough students in that one school to populate the whole village of Sun Prairie. Georgia may have felt overwhelmed by the changes, yet she was learning to adapt to them.

At the high school, Georgia took an art class taught by a strange, skinny woman who always wore a hat dripping with artificial violets. Georgia found it difficult to tear her eyes away from the amusing hat until that teacher began to show the students how to look carefully at objects in order to draw them. Georgia didn't like her one bit, but she admitted that the teacher made her become very aware of every detail.

Standing in front of the class the woman held up a fresh flower and demonstrated each part of the blossom. Once she brought in a Jack-in-the-pulpit, which Georgia had seen growing everywhere on the farm. Georgia drew the velvety purple flower from every angle and then began to experiment by drawing just one portion of the wildflower. In later years she drew the Jack over and over, varying its size and the intensity of its color. At first it was possible to recognize the flower, but with each variation its shape was simplified until it was no longer familiar. She had transformed it into a new form, an abstraction. This was a technique she would develop more fully in the future as she made repeated series of shells, shingles, the New Mexico hills.

When her junior year was over in Madison, Georgia joined her family in Williamsburg. Her first impression of the Southern town was its beauty and fragrance. She saw tall, spreading magnolias with shiny green leaves, flowers with a pungent lemony scent. Everywhere she noticed vines and trees growing profusely. There was flowering crape myrtle in many rosy shades. There were beech trees covered with thin, papery leaves and prickly balls, yellow dotted sassafras trees, flowering white dogwood, ancient gnarled mulberry trees, which had become havens for busy silkworms.

The family's handsome new home, Wheatland, was situated behind a thick hedge, covered with tall trellises of climbing flowers that reached the second-story porch. There were not enough pieces of furniture to fill all eighteen rooms, but the younger children loved playing in the near-empty house and huge attic. Georgia was especially pleased with the fireplaces she found in almost every room.

The O'Keeffe family home in Williamsburg, Virginia.
Colonial Williamsburg Photograph

Francis opened a grocery store that stocked many of the items he had previously grown on his farm. Among tall stacks of tinned goods there were also delicacies like green turtle meat, oysters, and sardines. There were baskets filled with dried apricots and prunes, fresh fruits and vegetables, seed potatoes, and onion sets. There were boxes of candles, soap, scrub brushes. Bins along the wall contained sugar and salt, garden seed and starch. Purchases were wrapped in crinkly brown paper torn from a huge roll on the counter.

Their proper Southern neighbors did not know what to make of the newcomers, especially when they were as different as the O'Keeffes seemed to be. Southern gentlemen did not work at trade as Francis did in his store, nor did they labor on farms and property as Francis had always done.

Eventually Ida was accepted, and it seemed to help that her family came from Hungarian nobility and that she could prove it with the treasures and jewels her father had brought with him from Hungary.

The townspeople saw Georgia as an unusual, artistic type who wouldn't conform to the dress and behavior expected of Southern girls her age. After two years on her own, Georgia had become independent and sure of herself. She wasn't concerned about

25

what others thought of her and probably enjoyed shocking the neighbors with her long daily walks at dawn and her tailored, no nonsense clothing. Nothing was going to prevent Georgia from watching the colors created by the rising sun, and she was quick to admit that she liked the world early in the morning and without any people.

5

"Georgie" at Chatham

GEORGIA'S SIXTEENTH BIRTHDAY (in the fall of 1903) was celebrated at Chatham Episcopal Institute, a girls' boarding school several hundred miles from Williamsburg. At one time the school had been a large private home atop a wooded hill, its many windows facing the distant Blue Ridge Mountains. The interior was not as luxurious as its setting. The floors were rough and mostly unpainted. The students studied by the light of kerosene lamps and were warmed by small wood-burning stoves in each room. They took weekly baths and shared the outdoor outhouse.

Georgia made the art studio her special place at Chatham. She worked there as though it belonged to her, freely spreading and splashing the paint for her watercolors without concern that it splattered the walls and floor. At other times, Georgia worked with delicate concentration despite having only rough paper and awkwardly large brushes. Once she created a lilac bouquet composed of layer upon layer of tiny blossoms so real that the painting seemed to have its own fragrance.

A small watercolor called *Pansies* was given to her friend, Susan Young, as a graduation gift. It is one of the rare works saved from her early years because Georgia destroyed the rest, telling her friends she did not want to be embarrassed by her student work later when she became famous. Chatham kept Georgia's painting of red and yellow corn, which was considered her best work of the year, displaying it proudly until the building burned down many years later.

By the time Georgia was at Chatham she had been studying art for almost five years. Her extraordinary talent soon become obvious to her classmates and to Mrs. Elizabeth Mae Willis, who was both principal and art instructor at Chatham. Mrs. Willis was also an accomplished artist who gave the greatest gift of all to Georgia—the freedom in which to grow and create on her own. She encouraged Georgia to spend time in the studio when other students were at study hall and did not force her to produce work when Georgia did not feel up to it.

Chatham Episcopal Institute prior to 1906.
Courtesy Chatham Hall

Alice, I' wish you would
please show me the
third oil stove if you
know where it is.

O'Keeffe.

Young ladies H₂S have a
very disagreeable
odor

Georgia's caricatures of teachers, *Mortar Board Yearbook,*
1905.
Courtesy Chatham Hall

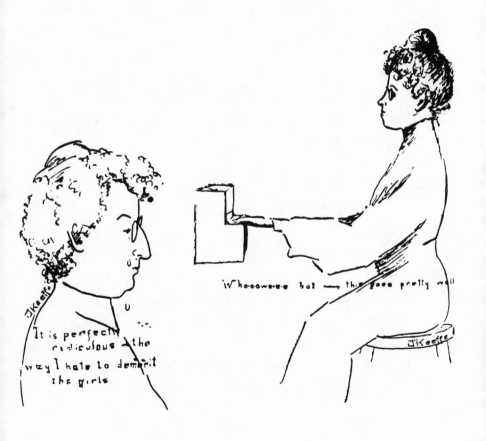

At first her classmates hardly knew what to make of Georgia. They, too, were startled by her plain, almost severely tailored clothes, when their outfits were covered with frills and bows. They continued to tease her at every opportunity about the time she had been mistaken for a housemaid because of her simple dress. But she quickly became a favorite when she revealed another, more mischievous side of her personality. Then she was "Georgie," leading them in pranks or teaching them to play poker.

Georgia drew amusing and accurate caricatures of her teachers and her classmates, many of which were included in Chatham's *Mortar Board Yearbook*. She was chosen art editor of that book, and in it is a rhyme to describe her:

> *O is for O'Keeffe; an artist divine*
> *Her paintings are perfect and her drawings are fine.*

Every afternoon Georgia joined her classmates for hikes in the Virginia hills. They walked single file behind the teacher, exploring the trails and inhaling the scent of the trees. After they returned from the compulsory walk, Georgia usually inveigled a friend to take a second walk, even though it was against the rules. She knew she would be given demerits if she

Georgia, as she appeared in the Chatham yearbook, *Mortar Board*, 1905.
Courtesy Chatham Hall

Calisthenics, Georgia's drawing for the *Mortar Board Yearbook*, 1905.
Courtesy Chatham Hall

was caught and would have to spend Saturdays working them off, but it was worth it. The outdoors was always a tonic for Georgia. She said the distance called out to her and made her feel more alive than when she was cooped up in mythology, physiology, or French classes.

On graduation day, when she and the six other young women were being honored, she told the audience of parents and friends that she almost hadn't been able to join the graduating class. She had had to repeat the spelling test six times before she passed it, and she predicted spelling would always be a problem for her in the future.

In 1938, at the age of fifty, Georgia received an Honorary University Degree from the College of William and Mary in Williamsburg. She found it humorous that she should be so honored since her spelling had not improved one bit. She must also have been aware of the irony that both her brothers had been able to attend William and Mary, while she, as a woman, could not.

6

Chicago Art Institute

THERE WERE educational restrictions on women in
the United States from its earliest years. Until the
mid-1800s young women could not attend most colleges or universities, except during special summer
sessions. Art schools were also closed to them. Gradually, the situation improved with the development
of fine women's colleges and increased coeducational
opportunities. Art schools also opened their doors to
women. One liberal art academy allowed men and
women to study together from the same plaster casts
as long as a fig leaf covered the male sexual organs.
Eventually women were permitted to draw from the
live model, as long as they were segregated from
male students.

The prevailing attitude was that women should
receive basic training in the arts and music, just as

they learned to do stitchery, darning, and other handwork important to their future lives as wives and mothers. Georgia and her sisters were fortunate that their mother wanted them to become more than proper young ladies. Georgia's grandmothers had been strong, determined women who worked hard and yet were never too busy to appreciate the beauty in their surroundings. They became models for the O'Keeffe aunts and sisters to emulate.

Georgia did not need much persuasion when her mother and Mrs. Willis encouraged her to continue studying art. While they may have expected her to become a fine art teacher, she herself was fully committed to her early decision to become an artist. In the fall of 1905, when she was almost eighteen, Georgia packed her valise and took the train to Chicago. She moved in with Ida's brother, her uncle Charles, and sister, Aunt Ollie, who lived within walking distance of the Art Institute.

Aunt Ollie had been a lively young woman with a great sense of independence, who served as another strong model for Georgia. Ollie told her to strive for her goals, even when they seemed difficult to attain. If she, Ollie, could break barriers, working as the only woman proofreader on a large city newspaper, Georgia could do it, too.

For years Georgia had heard about the famous

Chicago Art Institute, which exhibited its fine European paintings and sculpture and provided excellent classes. When she set out to register one morning, she was amazed to see the immense building, framed against the sky, with the blue expanse of nearby Lake Michigan. Madison High School had once seemed a large building to Georgia, but next to the Art Institute, it was dwarfed. The Institute spread along several city blocks. At each end of its broad stairway, stately bronze lions stood poised, ready to step right off their pedestals. Their shiny tails, gracefully arched, were kept polished by small, adventurous children sliding along them.

Georgia entered the massive doors with the same sense of adventure. While she waited for her locker and her drawing supplies, she could see that see was younger than most of the other women. She felt conspicuous, like a "child with her long black braid and big black bow." But not for long.

On the first day of class she was too busy concentrating on her work to worry about her youth. New students were sent into the shadowy gallery rooms crowded with plaster casts of figures. She was told to draw the torso of an armless man. As she worked, another student kept coming over to watch what she was doing. Georgia decided to see what his sketch looked like. She found his easel and saw that he was using dark, tight lines and very heavy shading as he copied the statue before him. He kept telling Georgia that his was the right way to draw. She was quickly assigned to a more advanced class in recognition of her ability, while the young man remained where he was. Georgia must have felt grateful to Sister Angelique who had taught her to soften and expand her lines.

Georgia continued to copy from casts in the museum and, with the other women students, began an anatomy class in a drab, olive-green basement room. When they were all assembled at their easels, the instructor asked the model to appear. Georgia could hardly believe her eyes. She knew she was blushing. She felt her face and neck grow warm with embarrassment as she tried to pay attention to the lesson.

Georgia had never been uncomfortable with her brothers and their male friends at the swimming hole. But this was different. Here were all the young women fully clothed and then covered in smocks while the nearly nude model was set forth in front of them to be studied. It didn't help her that the women were taught separately from the men. After that, Georgia forced herself to attend the weekly class because she knew it was expected of her, but she didn't care a bit for anatomy or all the scientific names given to parts of the body.

In her later work she would not use human models or paint the people in her life. She found natural forms the most satisfying models. She gained valuable insight into all living forms from John Vanderpoel's lectures on drawing the human figure. His classes were held in an upstairs room as light and airy as the basement anatomy room had been dreary. With black and white crayon Vanderpoel drew large figures on tan paper, while at the same time he told the students how to best show the curve of the shoulder or the grace of the wrist and fingers. Georgia absorbed his lines and words and later treasured his book, *The Human Figure.*

Instructors at the Art Institute rated students in their classes every month in the same way European art schools did. Competition for top ratings was fierce because promotion was based on class standings, as was location of seating next to casts or models. The higher the rating, the better the view. Georgia was rated the best student in Vanderpoel's life drawing class of twenty-nine women, and she also did very well in her other classes.

When the school year came to an end, Georgia was more than ready to return to the fresh, clean air of the Virginia countryside. She had no idea that a typhoid epidemic caused by bacteria-infested water was raging there. After several weeks at home, Georgia became one of its victims. She was very ill, hovering between life and death throughout the long, humid summer months. When her body wasn't burning with fever it was shaking with chills, which layers of quilts did not remedy. Her head never stopped aching and the fever filled her mind with terrors.

7

"Patsy" at the League

AFTER THREE MONTHS of illness, Georgia was left too weak to lift her head from the pillow. Gradually she could sit up for short periods, but the first time she saw herself in a looking glass she was frightened by her thin, wan face. To her horror, she also saw that her thick hair had fallen out in hunks during the fever. She covered her head with a lace cap to conceal her baldness from her own eyes and to avoid shocking others.

As her energy slowly returned, Georgia was able to spend more time outdoors. For her, the fragrance of a late-blooming rose was as curative as any medicine. That fall the elm leaves seemed more vivid than ever, the lavender beauty berries glowed, and the majestic magnolias were splendidly decorated by their scarlet cones. The crisp air soothed her and brought color to her pale skin. Her hair began to grow back in soft curls around her face.

She spent the rest of the year working at her easel, often setting it outside to capture the landscape. Mrs. Willis, Chatham's principal, frequently came to visit and always pressed Georgia to think about continuing her art education at the Art Students League in New York, where she herself had been a student. Georgia felt well enough to think about going back to school, but she worried that her father's business was not bringing in enough money to support the whole family. She had even started to apply for a teaching position when her parents assured her they could manage to send her for further study. That was all she needed to hear. She put her art supplies together, packed her shirtwaists and toiletries into a valise, and was ready for the long train ride to New York.

On the journey, Georgia had time to sort out her feelings as she watched all the small towns and stations whiz past. Some of the tiny cottages seemed close enough for her to touch and made her realize what a different life she had chosen from the families living inside. She was excited by what awaited her, but as she transferred to the ferry for the final stretch of the trip, she began to feel uneasy. This time there were no relatives waiting at the ferry slip to bustle her off to their home. Instead, she had to rely on herself and on help from colorful New Yorkers, who gave their directions in accents unlike the Southern drawl she had recently known.

The streets of New York were thick with people at all times of day and night. Vendors offered everything from hot chestnuts to fresh dates and "ersters." On every corner small urchins were hawking newspapers or shoeshines. The roadways were crowded with swaying double-decker buses, smaller open buses, electric trolleys, elegant broughams drawn by handsome horses, or drays pulled by nags.

The League, on West 57th Street, provided her with rental listings from which she found a room in a nearby boarding house for a few dollars a week. Once she was settled, she found life in New York exhilarating, and the other students quickly adopted her as their pet. They regarded her as a vivacious, curly-headed young woman whom they nicknamed "Patsy" to go with her Irish family name. She attended parties and dances given by the students and always stood out next to the other young women whose long tresses were kept piled in high smooth pompadours.

One of Georgia's favorite classes was a still life class taught by William Merritt Chase. He appeared weekly—dressed as a dandy in his tall hat, spats on

Still Life with Hare, 1908. Oil. Georgia's prize-winning painting
from her student days at the Art Students' League of
New York.
The Art Students' League of New York

his shoes, a flower in his lapel—to look at the students' paintings through his glasses, which hung from a cord around his neck. He arranged the items to be painted, such as brass and copper pots, fruits, vegetables, and flowers, and then demanded a new painting every day, each one to be done over the last, each alive and exciting. He was a strict taskmaster.

From Chase she learned to paint quickly and deftly and won first prize for her still life of a dead rabbit lying next to a copper pot. She was also made class monitor, which meant that she was considered one of the best pupils.

Eugene Speicher, a handsome older student at the League, wanted to paint Georgia and kept asking her to pose for him. She wasn't interested and continually refused his requests, telling him she was eager to do her own work.

He continued to taunt her, saying that she would never become a great painter like he was going to be. She would just end up teaching at some school for girls.

Eventually Georgia did sit for him and the portrait won Eugene Speicher a fifty dollar prize and was later reproduced in the League's catalogue.

Georgia was tempted to pose regularly because students were paid one dollar for a four-hour portrait class. She weighed the choices in her notebook,

Eugene Speicher, *Portrait of Georgia O'Keeffe*, 1908. Oil on oval panel, 17 x 11".
The Art Students' League of New York (Paul Juley, original photographer)

listing all the advantages and disadvantages. Her final decision was that painting had to come first if she was to succeed. She realized she was beginning to take herself and her work seriously.

Georgia had been searching for ways to express herself since she was a young girl in her Wisconsin tower room. Her fascination with the brightness of sunlight, moonlight, and starlight had begun even earlier. Now she left the League's classrooms to capture new scenes that intrigued her. She painted the moon's glow on a group of poplar trees standing tall against the evening sky and mirrored in the nearby Hudson River.

Another night painting, which she considered her best, was done during a summer visit to Lake George in upstate New York. From the edge of the lake, Georgia captured birch trees whose bark reflected the moon shining against the damp, mysterious marshes.

While Georgia needed to work in solitude, she also enjoyed excursions with the other students. On a brisk afternoon in January, she joined a group going to Alfred Stieglitz's gallery at 291 Fifth Avenue. They tramped playfully through the snow before crowding into a tiny elevator which pulled them by rope the four flights up to the gallery.

Stieglitz was exhibiting work done by the French

sculptor Rodin, which was different than any previously shown in the United States. The instructors
at the League were very critical of Rodin's drawings,
calling them meaningless scribbles. Stieglitz was used
to that kind of controversy. For years he had been
presenting work of photographers, painters, and
sculptors that was new and unusual. His gallery had
become a meeting place where those artists and their
friends came together to discuss, to question, and to
share their concerns about the changes taking place
in the art world.

That day the students came prepared for heated
discussion with the opinionated Stieglitz. They
crowded into one of the gallery's small rooms and
began to challenge him about Rodin's drawings. He
insisted they were not mere blobs of color, but advanced, abstract ways to visualize the body. With
bold gestures he defended their artistic value. His
gray hair grew more disheveled, his eyes blazed, his
bushy mustache never stopped moving. Georgia
kept backing away from the passionate talk until she
ended up in the adjoining room. She could not participate with the others and was unmoved by what
she saw in Rodin's small, sketchy figures. She felt
they "didn't look like anything I had been taught
about drawing." No wonder it was suggested that
Rodin had created the drawings with his eyes shut.

Georgia returned once again to Stieglitz's gallery—called "291"—to see another exhibit of abstract drawings done by the Frenchman, Matisse. They were as startling to her as the Rodin drawings had been. One art critic, Chamberlain, noted the Matisse drawings were "likely to go quite over the head of the ordinary observer—or under his feet." He felt the "female figures . . . of an ugliness most appalling."

At the League, Georgia had been learning to work in the classical method, portraying objects as they looked, with accurate perspective and realistic colors. She was not quite ready to understand the directions the European artists were taking as they forced the viewer to use imagination and supply missing lines or incomplete ideas. Georgia would eventually also break with tradition as she developed confidence in her own work.

By the time school was over for the summer, Georgia felt quite comfortable with her life in New York. She prepared for a short visit to Virginia, unaware that she would not return to the League.

8

Teaching in Texas

Georgia was greeted at home by her father with the news that he had closed his grocery store and that none of his other business ventures had succeeded. He was despondent over his financial problems and the fact that he could no longer finance her education.

Georgia tried to console her father, but her own feelings of disappointment were difficult to conceal. For years she had been determined to become an artist. Working at the League brought her one step closer. Now she would have to give it all up and go to work to support herself. She felt she could not work on her painting part time. It was all or nothing. With great sadness she packed away her dream with her art supplies.

She moved back to Chicago, where she found a

job in an advertising company, producing sketches for newspapers and magazines, sometimes drawing intricate designs of lace and embroidery for fashion ads. She was able to work very quickly, a skill she'd been taught by William Chase at the League, but she felt no satisfaction in producing advertising copy. It was just a job. She kept at it for two years until a case of measles left her eyes weakened and forced her to give up the exacting work. At the age of twenty-three, she returned to live with her family.

Again, Mrs. Willis came to visit Georgia. Her affection for her former student had never diminished and she still hoped Georgia would find a way to continue developing her artistic talent. Mrs. Willis asked Georgia to take over for her at Chatham for several weeks. Returning to her boarding school was a pleasant experience, since Georgia had spent many happy moments at the school. Yet in the back of her mind she may have recalled Speicher's warning that she was fated to become merely a teacher at a girls' school.

Her family was resettled in Charlottesville, where her father had opened a creamery, and her mother was running a boarding house. Ida was trying to maintain cheerful spirits as she took care of family and boarders, despite the fact that *she* had now come down with tuberculosis. Georgia's four sisters were all living at home; Ida and Anita began attending summer school classes at the University of Virginia.

After her first few art classes, Anita could hardly wait to tell Georgia about her drawing professor, Alon Bement. She insisted Georgia should come to class to meet him and see how he taught the students to use basic geometric shapes with which to create designs. No one had to feel intimidated if he could not reproduce an actual landscape or parts of the human figure. His ideas were based on theories developed by his colleague, Arthur Wesley Dow.

Georgia found in Bement's and Dow's concepts a whole new way to approach art. She enrolled in Bement's advanced drawing class and immediately produced quantities of unusual work. It seemed her creative energy had been waiting for just such an outlet. Bement recognized her outstanding talent and selected her to be his teaching assistant at the college the following summer.

To support herself during the year, Georgia accepted the job of Drawing Supervisor in Amarillo, Texas. In August, 1912, she set off, her enthusiasm making up for the teaching experience she lacked. "What I knew about teaching was like going to the moon," she remarked later. She could hardly wait to reach Texas. It had held an appeal since she was a child listening to her mother read adventure stories that romanticized the West.

The reality of Amarillo was quite different. She found a dusty, arid cattle town into which thousands of longhorn cattle were led before being sent by railroad to the rest of the country. The cattle were tightly packed into wooden pens near the station. Night and day the air echoed with their cries—the calves bawling for their mothers, the mothers crying for their calves.

Georgia boarded in a hotel where she took meals with the hard-working cattlemen, who devoured huge amounts of food and offered little conversation. She witnessed an actual shooting, heard many other stories about outlaws and rustlers. But for Georgia the appeal of Amarillo came when she explored beyond the wooden sidewalks of town, past the saloons, the hotels, and the people. She could not locate a leaf or a green blade of grass, and the largest tree she could find was no bigger than her wrist, but near the riverbed she came upon the yellow earth that gave the town its Spanish name. She reveled in the flatness of that land, which allowed her to see for miles in every direction. And she quickly learned to read the weather signals from the vast sky.

She learned how disastrous that weather could

be when powerful winds overturned the few Model
Ts in town or violent sheets of brown dust covered
everything along their path. Yet in summer she re-
lished being able to sit outside during the night to
watch displays of heat lightning, and she always rose
in time to marvel at how the plains were transformed by dawn's colors.

Georgia was inspired by the bleakness and energy of the land, and she conveyed her positive feelings to her students. They were loving young people
whose lack of material wealth did not prevent them
from being very open to her teachings. She fought
against using the art textbook from which they were
supposed to copy because it was full of ornate items
they had never seen. How on earth could they be expected to copy such things, thought Georgia. Instead
she had them sketch objects from their environment—a pebble or a hunk of ragweed. She also
posed problems for them as Bement had done in his
classes, having them divide the space of a large
square to make a pleasant or interesting design. She
told them Bement's theory that you should "Fill a
space in a beautiful way." Everything you do in life—
the way you write a letter, fix your hair, place objects
in your room—can be done with thoughtfulness and
beauty.

Georgia spent two exhilarating years teaching in

Georgia at twenty-seven, when she taught at the University
of Virginia. July, 1915.
Holsinger Studio Collection, University of Virginia Library

Amarillo, learning and growing all the time. Speicher's words could no longer frighten her. In the summers she returned to Charlottesville to assist Bement at the University of Virginia, always feeling grateful to him for getting her back on her artistic course. She later wrote, "I wouldn't be arting now if it wasn't for him."

9

"... Her colors were always the brightest"

Bement appreciated whatever Georgia painted, whether it was a realistic canvas of hollyhocks from her yard or an abstract design created by a tent flap she had noticed on a camping trip. He felt she should trust her inner feelings about her work, but he also kept her in touch with the latest ideas that were developing in the New York art world.

There had been a major Armory Show in 1913, which presented a large number of startling avant-garde works done by young European and American artists. One writer called it the introduction of "modern art to a bewildered American public ... " Alfred Stieglitz had been attempting to do the same thing on a small scale at his Gallery 291 for years.

Following the Armory Show, Picasso, Rodin, Matisse, Cézanne, and many other sculptors and painters became familiar names to a broader segment in New York.

Bement never stopped urging Georgia to return to New York for further study and stimulation. Georgia finally listened to him and enrolled at Columbia Teachers College in 1914. She found a small room in which to live, kept it almost bare except for a bright red geranium set on the fire escape outside her window.

Georgia was a serious student, hungry to learn as much as possible about artistic methods. She hardly studied the other required subjects and no longer went dancing with friends because the late nights left her too weary to concentrate on her work the following morning.

Georgia became very close to a friendly, vivacious young student, Anita Pollitzer. Together they were allowed to paint behind a screen while the other students were required to continue working from casts. Anita knew even then that Georgia "was different . . . Her colors were always the brightest, her palette the cleanest, her brushes the best— though to accomplish this she would do without much else."

She and Anita shared a love for music as well as

art. They attended concerts together and often traveled arm in arm to Stieglitz's gallery to see which show he was presenting.

Alfred Stieglitz was a passionate photographer who also thought of himself as a teacher. Throughout his career he had tried to introduce the latest ideas and concepts in art. He used his own photography, presented the work of other artists in his gallery, and lectured and prodded everyone who would listen.

Stieglitz roamed the city seeking inspiration for his photographs. He snapped a range of subjects, from the changing of horses on a horse car during a snowstorm to the emotional scene of immigrants in steerage as they arrived from Europe.

Stieglitz's technical knowledge of the chemistry of photography enabled him to capture scenes in rain, snow, and the dark of night. For one of his snow scenes he waited three hours in a storm until everything came together perfectly for his shot. Eventually he was to convince museums that photography was an art form as valid as any other, and most experts agreed that Stieglitz and his Gallery 291 had a very important influence on art.

The gallery and the man would certainly have an influence on Georgia. At 291 she saw artists selling work they had exhibited. In magazines she read about other artists making a living from their art. When one of her pictures was published in a respected art magazine, she said to herself there was no reason why she could not paint canvases that people would want to buy.

10

Discoveries in Charcoal

GEORGIA returned to teach summer school at the University of Virginia in 1915, eager to share her growing enthusiasm for modern art with her students. She had spent the fall months in New York, where she had been exposed to works by Picasso, Cézanne, and Matisse at Stieglitz's gallery.

She told the students how Cézanne in his late work no longer copied each detail of the flowers, vase, and background of a still life. Rather, with a few delicate brush strokes he could suggest an exquisitely fragrant bouquet. Matisse was no longer drawing the body with exact anatomical lines. Instead, his figures had become flowing lines that distorted their shape and startled the viewer.

Georgia explained that people did not always understand why these European artists were breaking with traditions of the past. She read her students articles from Stieglitz's fine journal, *Camera Work*, and other magazines describing what the artists were trying to do and the impact their work would have on American art.

Georgia had become friendly with Arthur Macmahon, a serious young professor from Columbia University who was interested in politics and government. They often took long walks together in the lush Virginia hills. The feel of cold water on bare feet, the touch of leaves, grass, and flowers, was a refreshing change from the classroom for both of them. In the fall, they parted when Arthur returned to teach in New York.

GEORGIA was again faced with conflicts over what she would do for the coming year. She knew she had to find a job to support herself, yet when she worked she found she was unable to concentrate fully on her art. At the very last moment she accepted a college teaching position at Columbia in South Carolina, because she would have to teach only four classes a week and could devote her free time to painting.

After a short time at the school, Georgia realized how little she had in common with the other teachers and the young women students who were preparing to become music teachers. She felt isolated, without friends who could share her interest in the outdoors or discuss the latest art news. Fortunately, Anita, her friend from Columbia Teachers College, wrote almost every day, providing anecdotes about their former teachers and friends in New York. Arthur Macmahon also kept in close touch and gave her something to look forward to when he promised to visit during Thanksgiving weekend.

They spent a wonderful holiday together and before he left, Arthur asked Georgia to marry him. It seemed the perfect answer for her. She thought she loved Arthur and welcomed the financial security marriage would provide. It meant she would never have to teach again. But the more she thought about it, the more her inner voice told her it was wrong; that marriage was not for her. She was going to become an artist and had to follow a different path than most other women. She remembered how totally absorbed her mother had been by rearing children and running the household. Georgia did not want to give up her independence or her dream. She refused Arthur's marriage proposal. But it left her feeling more alone than ever, and she sank into a deep depression.

She found that painting no longer soothed her as it had in the past. She was dissatisfied with everything she tried to create. She began to study her recent work and decided the paintings were imitations, reflecting more the influence of her teachers than anything else. She saw Bement's style in one picture, Chase's in another, Dow's in a third. Where was Georgia O'Keeffe? She had to admit that others already painted as well as she could. It was not enough for her to copy what had been done.

She put away her paintings. She packed up her watercolors and oils, the fine brushes she had treasured. She was going to begin anew, using only charcoal, in a search for her own style.

There were many shapes in her head—shapes she had never seen anywhere. Night after night she worked in a frenzy, going deep into herself, into the visions in her mind. She put sheets of paper on the floor and drew the shapes until her fingers ached. Still the ideas poured out of her. She worried that she might be losing her mind, but she could not stop. "I wonder if I'm a raving lunatic for trying to make these things," she wrote to Anita. At last she was drained of ideas. She had to know what Anita thought. She made a roll of the drawings, stuck them in a mailing tube, and sent them to New York, cautioning Anita not to show them around.

When Anita received the drawings she took them into a classroom, locked the door behind her, and spread them all around the room. She studied them for a long time, feeling overwhelmed by their power and originality. There were unusual shapes churning together, their energy resounding from the paper. Anita could not believe how alive they seemed. She remembered something Georgia had once written her: "Anita—do you know I believe I would rather have Stieglitz like something—anything I had done—than anyone else I know of."

Anita rolled the drawings back into their tube, and for two weeks she kept them to herself, as Georgia had requested. But she could stand it no longer, so one afternoon she set out to take them to Gallery 291. When she arrived, the elevator was out of order. Not stopping to catch her breath, she climbed the many stairs.

Stieglitz was alone in the gallery at the end of a long Saturday. It was January first, his fifty-second birthday. He was pleased to see Anita, but even her exuberant personality could not erase his sense of weariness. She handed him the mailing tube and urged him to look at what she had brought him, no matter how tired he felt.

He removed the tightly rolled sheets, leaned back against the wall, and began to examine each drawing. Then, without saying a word, he started all over again.

Anita watched as his eyes scrutinized the curves and fluid lines of Georgia's work. Through the overhead skylight she noticed daylight fading into twilight. The only sound in the room came from the rustling of Georgia's drawings.

It seemed like hours before Stieglitz spoke. "Finally, a woman on paper . . . these are the purest, finest, sincerest things that have entered 291 in a long while."

11

Drawings on Display

Anita almost flew down the stairs when she left Stieglitz. She could hardly wait to write Georgia telling her what she had done. Georgia responded that she was grateful for Anita's courage in taking the drawings to Stieglitz. She herself would never have been able to do it. She also told her friend how pleased she was to have "said something" to Anita and to Stieglitz. Then she wrote to Stieglitz telling him that "Words and I—are not good friends at all ..." but she had to know what he really thought about her drawings.

Stieglitz found it easy to write and spent many hours each day corresponding with his friends in long, rambling letters, just as if he were speaking to them. But his response to Georgia's plea was short and to the point. He would wait to tell her his reactions in person. For the time being, he could reassure her that she was doing valuable work.

Receiving Stieglitz's approval gave Georgia the courage to continue. As she confided to Anita, ". . . it makes me want to keep on—and I had almost decided it was a fool's game."

In March, Georgia became impatient with the situation in South Carolina, resigned her teaching position, and returned to New York to study with Dow at Teachers College. Anita asked her aunt and uncle to let Georgia live with them so that she would be able to manage on her small savings. After life in a small Southern community, Georgia found New York more stimulating than ever. She traveled back and forth from classes, to Stieglitz's gallery, and to her room in a jubilant state.

Stieglitz decided to hang ten of Georgia's charcoals in early summer, without her knowledge or permission. One day a student at the College casually mentioned she'd seen an exhibit at 291 by a "Virginia O'Keeffe." When Georgia rushed to the Gallery, she was disturbed to discover her drawings displayed on the burlap-covered walls. She had thought of them as her intimate visions and was uncomfortable having them exposed to public view. Stieglitz did not recognize her. He saw a thin young woman, dressed in black except for a small white collar. After she introduced herself, he explained that he had no choice but to hang her work; the drawings were an important development for the art world. He told her that it was the first time an American woman had been able to express her feelings honestly in an abstract way on paper.

Many people came to 291 to see the controversial drawings for themselves. They all buzzed about the energy, the erotic, or sexual, energy they found in her charcoal sketches. Stieglitz encouraged discussion, saying it was time for Americans to openly express their natural feelings about the body and its urges. He felt that society had been repressed far too long. When he saw the numbers of people coming to the gallery, he kept it open through July, when it would normally have closed.

None of the critics agreed when they described Georgia's charcoal drawings. One felt they were quite unrelated to nature, while another said they were definitely forms in nature.

There was no question that the flowing shapes had a life of their own. Some were jagged, others flamelike in their upward movement on the paper. Some resembled rounded forms growing naturally from her charcoal. In these and her later paintings, the lines and shapes often resemble lines of the body. The curves of the body and those found in nature are part of a universal or organic design.

Georgia knew that the ideas for her shapes were coming from deep within her. She thought people were foolish to read all sorts of sexual connotations into her drawings. If they had to explain her drawings that way, she shrugged her shoulders and tried to ignore them. Much later in life she would say, ". . . they're really talking about their own affairs."

That summer, Georgia was glad to get away from the controversy over her first show, even though she dreaded returning home to Charlottesville. Her mother had died in May after a long bout with tuberculosis. She knew the house would be filled with many sad memories and also that her mother's death would mean the final break-up of her family. The affection and respect she had felt for her father had gradually changed as she watched him fail at one business venture after another. She also found it pathetic that his fear of tuberculosis could not prevent it from striking his family—first his three brothers and then his wife, even after he had taken her away from the extremes of Wisconsin weather.

Georgia now received emotional support from Stieglitz, who wrote her very often. She welcomed his letters, saying, "They have been like fine cold water when you are terribly thirsty." He sent her photographs he had taken of her drawings on the gallery walls. They were valid proof that she had been presented to an important segment of the New York art world in 1916, when she was twenty-eight. If she doubted herself for a moment, she could look again at Stieglitz's photographs and see her work as it had actually been displayed. She had been recognized as an artist.

12

Support from Stieglitz

 EORGIA'S teaching position for fall took her to West Texas State Normal College in Canyon, a tiny town south of Amarillo. She was determined to teach the college students in her design and interior decorating classes to fill spaces in beautiful ways, as she had done with her younger students in Amarillo. She also tried to open their minds to writers of the time and to what modern artists, such as Picasso, were trying to accomplish in their work.

She still clomped about in sensible walking shoes and wore mainly black and white tailored clothing that she stitched herself. Georgia found the time she spent sewing was also precious time for thinking. While she completed a garment, she would work out design ideas for her classes or for a new painting.

Canyon provided Georgia with endless scenes

for her paintings. She could wrap herself in the changing colors and seasons of the sky and prairie. "The whole sky—and there is so much of it out here—was just blazing—and gray-blue clouds were rioting all through the hotness of it—" was how she described the setting in a letter to Anita.

Georgia began to express herself in paintings that used strong, simple forms with vibrant colors. Now that she had defined her unique style in the black and white charcoal drawings, she was able to use color even more powerfully than before. She often said that she thought in color the way others think in words. She also had the unusual ability to see in three dimensions—not just right to left, up and down, but going to and from the viewer "through the thickness of paper as well . . ."

While her younger sister, Claudia, lived with her, they would walk mile after mile along the prairie, watching the evening star change as sunset burst over it. Georgia painted the evening star repeatedly until she had ten bold watercolors. She also painted scenes of Palo Duro Canyon, with its boiling orange foam rising from the depths and coloring even the clouds above.

Her friends and fellow teachers in Canyon could not understand her work. When they looked at her paintings they might see shapes that were fa-

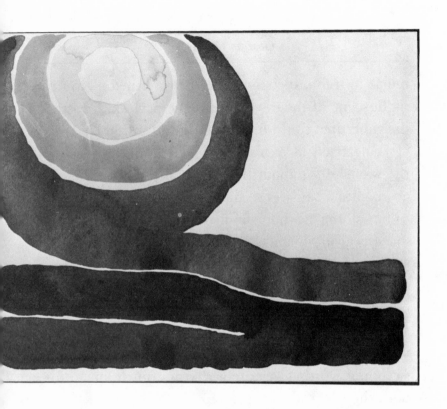

Evening Star III, 1917. Watercolor, 9 x 11⅞".
Collection, The Museum of Modern Art, New York, Mr. and Mrs.
Donald B. Straus Fund

miliar to them, such as a bright "watermelon" in her night scene of the town against the dark sky. Most of the time they could find nothing recognizable.

She tried to explain that her paintings showed the way she *felt* about the star or the canyon, but an acquaintance answered that she must have been sick to her stomach when she made them.

Because Stieglitz understood her work, she felt she could tell him her deepest feelings in the frequent letters she sent him. Both of them wrote a bold, sprawling script with black ink on crisp white sheets of bond. Georgia's ideas were separated with wavy lines rather than with commas, causing her sweeping words to create a rhythm on the page for both the eye and the ear.

In addition to sending letters, Georgia continued to mail Stieglitz rolls of drawings for his approval and, with them, Stieglitz began to plan a show for the following year. The show opened on April 3, 1917. A reviewer, Henry Tyrrell, called it "strange art," but he valued its technical quality and especially the emotion it expressed.

Three days later, the United States declared war against Germany, and Stieglitz was filled with despair. His family had come from Germany, he had studied photography there as a young man, and now he felt betrayed by the country. In despair he vowed to give up his gallery, his photography, his fine magazine, the work he was doing for modern art, everything.

Georgia impulsively decided to see her show in New York and to cheer Stieglitz. When she arrived at 291, the paintings were already down but Stieglitz rushed about rehanging her bold Texas watercolors and the subtle, almost Oriental work called *Blue Lines*. Her presence did improve Stieglitz's mood, and he was able to give her news that he had sold one of her paintings for four hundred dollars—a strong view of the train rushing into Canyon with smoke billowing from the engine. It was a fitting subject for her first sale, since she had spent a great part of her life on trains anticipating what the next destination might hold.

Georgia spent three lively days in New York with Stieglitz. He was struck by Georgia's natural beauty and the intensity of her personality as he watched her move about his gallery. For a short time he was able to forget his depression and become totally absorbed in photographing Georgia in and around her paintings; in profile, with her long, delicate fingers against her dark dress. Georgia was a serene model, who could remain quiet for the many minutes required by Stieglitz's large box camera with its glass plates, although she admitted it was not easy.

"In three minutes you could have more itchy spots on you than you could imagine."

Stieglitz's grandniece described how it felt to sit for her uncle Alfred:

> *The tall tripod, the large wooden box*
> *of the camera, the plates carefully*
> *inserted and removed, the delicate*
> *groan of the advancing and retreating*
> *lens as it was tuned into focus, the*
> *black muslin under which Uncle Alfred's*
> *head dived when at last he was ready,*
> *the wheeze of the shutter, and finally,*
> *my reprieve.*

Stieglitz felt that an ideal portrait was one made up of many pictures taken over a long period of time so that it would show the subject's gradual growth and change. Over the next twenty years he would continue to photograph Georgia until he had taken as many as three hundred pictures, all of which he considered a "composite portrait."

From those first photographs, Georgia could see herself as an attractive woman. She had learned to accentuate her large, expressive eyes by pulling her hair straight back to frame her strong face. She held her slim figure tall and erect, dressing only in the finest fabrics of silk and wool even when her styles were very plain and unadorned.

After her brief visit to New York, Georgia reluctantly returned to her teaching commitment in Canyon. That summer, she and Claudia traveled to the Colorado Rockies but were forced to detour through New Mexico. For Georgia, that detour was pure serendipity. In New Mexico she was to discover the brilliant light and rugged settings that would become a fixed magnet in her mind until she could finally return to the Southwest in 1929.

Claudia moved to another small Texas town to begin student teaching in the fall, and most of Georgia's male students began enlisting in military service. Everyone in town was involved in the war effort. Georgia could not deal with the idea of war and that, added to her loneliness without Claudia, prevented her from painting for months. She began to worry that Stieglitz would never exhibit her work again, that the war was changing everything. She was filled with new doubts about ever becoming an established artist.

13

Full-Time Artist

Now it was Stieglitz's turn to lift Georgia's spirits. He had recognized Georgia's immense talent when he saw her first drawings. It was not surprising that his friends called him a "racing man with an eye for a winner." In order to free her mind of all worries, he secured a financial loan for her, arranged for her to live in his niece Elizabeth's apartment, and then sent a young friend to Texas to bring Georgia back to New York, if that was what she really wanted.

Georgia was more than ready to leave Texas and eager to have time to paint without teaching responsibilities. She knew that Stieglitz's interest in her work would be a constant inspiration, and she accepted his aid with gratitude. A very relieved Stieglitz met her at Penn Station.

When her belongings arrived from Texas in a wooden barrel, she unpacked them and threw out all her old paintings because New York was to become her new subject. First she made paintings of the inside of her colorful orange and yellow studio; then she turned to the outside world, drawing the buildings, the East River scenes, gleaming night scenes, all large and powerful as she felt New York to be.

In the summer she traveled with Stieglitz to his family home at Lake George, where she found many peaceful country scenes to paint and the opportunity to work in the earth tending flowers and vegetables. Together they went boating on the lake every evening. At least once a week they climbed Prospect Mountain, from which they could see for many miles. On her own, Georgia swam and hiked the hills and flower-covered meadows.

In her work Georgia changed from realism to abstraction, moving easily between the two. She might think about an idea for months until she was ready to put it down on canvas. Then she would paint the object over and over again as she had done earlier with the Jack-in-the-pulpit. Now she would use this method with a wooden shingle she found on the ground at Lake George. After many different paintings the shingle became less and less recognizable, until it was only the idea of a shingle.

The City, New York Rooftops, c. 1929. Charcoal drawing,
24 9/16 x 18 13/16". Georgia captured a view of New York
during the time she lived high above the city.
The Fine Arts Museums of San Francisco, AFGA, Gift of Mrs.
Charlotte S. Mack, 1961

Red Hills and the Sun, Lake George, 1927. Oil on canvas, 27 x 32″. Even without color, the sun seems to blaze over the curving slopes in Georgia's scene.
The Phillips Collection, Washington, D.C.

In another Lake George painting, Georgia's hills are a brilliant crimson while the hot sun above is exploding in shades of gold and violet. The shimmering movement of her colors causes the scene to throb with feeling.

Back in New York, Georgia shut out everything from her life that did not relate to art. She worked for long hours at a time with intense concentration. Her glass palette was always kept neat and clean, the rich colors separate from each other, and a fresh brush reserved for every shade.

Gallery 291 closed its doors with an exhibition of Georgia's work. By 1921, Stieglitz was offered two top floor rooms of the Anderson Galleries on Park Avenue to display his early photographs of Georgia, taken in every possible pose, with her clothes on and without them. His great-niece would say they were taken by the "three loving eyes of Alfred and his camera." Those photographs convinced people that Stieglitz was very much in love with the handsome young artist. She became as much talked about as her paintings.

Georgia's feelings for Stieglitz had changed from fear to deep respect and then to love. She valued his knowledge about art and people and shared the high standards he set for his work. They both sought the finest materials—brushes, paper, paint,

Georgia O'Keeffe and Alfred Stieglitz at Lake George.
Courtesy Josephine B. Marks (© J.B. Marks)

photographic equipment—to be certain their work would endure.

They lived together openly, which caused a stir among the gossips, especially since Stieglitz was not yet divorced from his wife. Georgia convinced him not to worry about public reaction, and they wrapped themselves in voluminous black capes against the world and the weather.

14

Public Success

WHEN STIEGLITZ announced Georgia's show at the Anderson Gallery in 1923, people arrived in droves to see what all the talk was about. More women came than had ever visited the gallery before. Among the one hundred works exhibited were abstracts painted to music and luscious realistic fruits and flowers in warm red hues. Georgia's annual shows would continue to draw crowds no matter what she painted, no matter what was happening in the world, and no matter what the critics said.

Her paintings had tremendous appeal and began to sell in large numbers. Georgia found it difficult to part with them, and to avoid some of that pain she turned over to Stieglitz the responsibility of selecting "parents" for her creations. Stieglitz insisted that "I do want Georgia's paintings to have homes—real homes," but Georgia noticed that he often "tried to keep people from buying. His favorite word was 'no.' " There was no question that he could infuriate people when he refused to sell to them, or forced them to take one painting when they preferred another. It was only because he wanted to be sure that a painting was purchased for the right reason.

Stieglitz did not take commissions on the work he sold for Georgia and his other artists. He would not consider selling his own photographs. He saw himself as an educator bringing viewer and artist together. He required very little money to live and was willing to let his first wife and his family assist him so that he could devote his energies to art.

Georgia usually found Stieglitz the best judge of her work until she began painting her enormous flowers, and then even he was taken aback and wondered what she was going to do with them. But Georgia knew she had found a way to make busy New Yorkers stop and take notice. She would magnify the flowers rather than paint them in the delicate way that had been customary in the past. She would present one part of the flower. She would startle people.

She made portraits of the very dark pansy and black iris. She painted sunflowers, petunias, new

Two Jimson Weeds with Green Leaves and Blue Sky, 1938. Oil on canvas, 48 x 40".
Lent by the Utah Museum of Fine Arts, Collection of Marilyn Hite

Jack-in-the-pulpits, poppies, morning glories. And they did startle people. Again, some tried to read sexual meanings into her paintings, but she knew that the inner parts of the flower had served as her models: the pistil, the stamen, the curving stem, or rounded petal. Again, she would tell them it was their business if they wanted to search for other meanings in her flowers.

In 1925, Stieglitz presented another show, which included the work of six men and Georgia. In his review of that show, Edmund Wilson wrote, "America seems definitely to have produced a woman painter comparable to her best woman poets and novelists." Georgia was "very annoyed at being referred to as a 'woman artist' rather than an artist," although there may have been some consolation for her when she read Wilson's conclusion: "Georgia outblazes the other painters . . . "

In those days it was not easy for any woman to become a recognized artist. Louise Nevelson, the sculptor, had warned that the world will think of you as a "freak." Georgia herself remembered, "all the male artists I knew, of course, made it very plain that as a woman I couldn't hope to make it—I might as well stop painting."

One of Stieglitz's colleagues, Arthur Dove, was an exception. He was amazed by Georgia's early wa-

tercolors and told Stieglitz, "this girl is doing naturally what many of us fellows are trying to do, and
failing." The other men in Stieglitz's group eventually grew to respect Georgia, but at first they dis-
trusted her, did not expect her to succeed, found
her colors too bright, her paintings erotic. They felt
that "*for a woman* she was a pretty good painter but
that, by definition, what she created could not really
be on the same plane as the work of a man."

There were even whispers that without Stieglitz,
Georgia might not have been recognized at all.

She was able to win them over by her strong, independent personality, her concentrated work on
her own painting, the hours she spent hanging
shows for the gallery. Most important of all was the
success she was having with the public. Her bright
paintings were selling, and when she painted a picture of an old shanty at Lake George, using what she
called the "dirty colors" the men preferred, that
painting also sold immediately.

It was in December, 1924, when Stieglitz was
sixty and Georgia thirty-seven, that they took the
ferry from New York to New Jersey to be married
by a justice of the peace. By then they had been living together for some six years. Georgia agreed to
the marriage, but chose not to answer to the name
Mrs. Stieglitz. She insisted on retaining her individu-

My Shanty—Lake George, 1922. Oil on canvas, 20 x 27".
Georgia's dark-colored painting of her workplace proved to
the "men" that she could paint like they did.
The Phillips Collection, Washington, D.C.

ality and her name. "I've had a hard time hanging on to my name, but I hang on to it with my teeth. I like getting what I've got on my own." Her close friends and associates were beginning to call her O'Keeffe and eventually it would become the name most widely used.

Georgia still did not sign her paintings with any name at all. When she was pleased with a picture she might initial it on the back. She believed that the canvas itself would be identified as hers by its technique and subject matter. No one else would paint her scenes in the way she did. When someone asked her why she didn't sign her paintings, it is said that she responded with a biting, "Why don't you sign your face?"

Georgia could be sharp and unpleasant, impatient with people, almost as a protection against them. She frightened children, and she frightened many adults with her sharp comments. "The meaning is there on the canvas," she snapped at an interviewer. "If you don't get it, that's too bad. I have nothing more to say than what I painted."

Georgia cherished her privacy. She knew she had to devote her total energy to art if she was to continue producing meaningful work. She once told a writer, "Making a decision to do something and then doing it requires *not* doing a dozen other things."

Stieglitz, on the other hand, thrived on people. He was "on call for anyone who chose to participate in 'the experience' he was having. People of all kinds came from all parts of the world . . . Stieglitz would talk for hours, for entire days . . . to two or ten or twenty people." While he talked, Georgia was always alone and painting.

15

"Half Mad with Love"
for New Mexico

For a time Georgia and Stieglitz lived high above New York City in the new thirty-four story Shelton Hotel. Georgia painted the sights from her windows: the angular skyscrapers, surfaces glinting in sunlight, tiny windows sparkling like fireflies at night. For her the sky was almost lost as each new building rose, taller than the last.

Every summer the two of them traveled to the Stieglitz farmhouse at Lake George, where Georgia could rediscover the sky and the rural settings reminiscent of her youth. But once there, she was also surrounded by people—Stieglitz's large family and many friends who came for holidays. Georgia began to feel stifled by the sameness of the routine, the packing to leave New York, the packing to return to New York, always the same people, the same scenes to paint.

She kept thinking of the glimpses she'd caught of New Mexico on her trip with Claudia twelve years before. She remembered the great expanse of unbroken land vying with an endless sky as broad as any she had experienced. She remembered the air, the light, and the brilliant colors. She had to get back there.

Georgia could not convince Stieglitz to change his ways and travel to New Mexico with her. He had always resisted making changes in his life. He gave the excuse that at sixty-five, his health was not good enough for him to accompany Georgia, who was twenty-three years younger and could easily adapt to the high altitude. Georgia kept trying to persuade him, but she finally realized she would have to make the trip without him.

She spent that first summer of 1929 in Taos, an artists' community in northern New Mexico. Years later she tried to explain what the desert meant to her, how it allowed her to see all around herself, with the light making "everything close and it is never, never the same. Sometimes the light hits the mountains from behind and front at the same time . . . so that you have distances in layers."

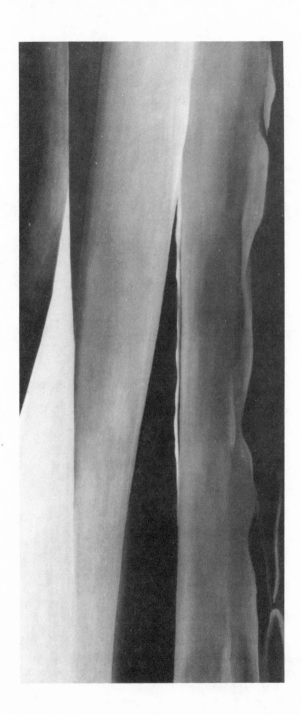

"Untitled" (desert abstraction), 1931. Oil on canvas, 15½ x 36½". This painting is considered a very early example of abstract work, which Georgia completed shortly after she began visiting the Southwest. Courtesy Museum of New Mexico

Ranchos Church, 1930. Oil on canvas, 24 x 36". Georgia often painted this early Spanish church. Her curving lines bring life to its warm adobe walls.
The Phillips Collection, Washington, D.C.

Along the road to Taos, Georgia found the ancient Ranchos de Taos Church, which she painted from every angle. She captured its smooth adobe-colored walls, its bulk, its sense of history. In one painting she set only the bulging corner of the church against the sky, saying that she found her fragments produced statements as strong, if not stronger, than a complete picture could.

The Ranchos de Taos Church as it appears today.
Charles Gherman, Photographer

The sun-bleached animal bones and skulls she found on the desert seemed to have sprouted from a land without flowers. Georgia didn't think of them in terms of death; rather, she saw them as symbols of longevity and survival.

She painted the bones floating in the sky as though they were surveying the territory. She peered through their openings with the same delight she had savored and eaten around the doughnut hole when she was a child. What she saw through the openings was a new dimension of the world. The sky became a mysterious setting, colors quivered against each other, light became more intense. On her return to New York in the fall, she brought along a barrel of bones and enough visions of the rich and vivid landscape to use throughout the year.

Georgia continued to return to New Mexico almost every summer, although Stieglitz never got used to her leaving. He finally admitted that he knew what an inspiration the area was for her work and that it was his sacrifice for her and for art to get along without her.

In 1938, Stieglitz suffered a severe heart attack, and both he and Georgia were aware that his health was not the same after that. He continued to work at his gallery, to see colleagues, to assist his biographer, to write his long letters; but he continued to have coronary pain, off and on, until he died in July, 1946.

Georgia had retained her independence within the marriage, but after his death, she missed Stieglitz, the closeness they had shared, the response to each other's work, the support she had been able to offer as he grew older.

She spent several years organizing his photographs and the artists' work he had collected, in order to donate and distribute it to various museums and libraries. Once that work was complete, Georgia felt there was nothing to hold her in New York, and she made New Mexico her permanent home. She toured the area on foot, on horseback, even learned to drive a Model A Ford wildly around the rolling hills. Sometimes she worked inside the car. To capture a bit of shade during the intense summer heat, she might slip under the car. To protect herself from the chill of winter, she bundled in layers of clothing and spread a carpet on the ground before setting up her easel.

She thought of New Mexico as a lonely but beautiful land. "Sometimes I think I'm half mad with love for this place. I've climbed and poked into every hill and mountain in sight." ". . . That's my backyard," she said pointing to an enormous cliff towering over a canyon.

The White Place in Shadow, 1940. Oil on canvas, 30 x 24".
Massive rock formations near Abiquiu which Georgia found
pleasing. She softened the lines with touches of shrubbery on
the bottom and top edges.
The Phillips Collection, Washington, D.C.

For several years Georgia stayed at Ghost Ranch, south of Taos. She avoided interacting with most of the guests at the dude ranch, but she worked hard to befriend the land. For her, the rugged hills at Ghost Ranch were a challenge physically and artistically. She painted them over and over. She climbed up them on foot and on horseback. If the horse grew weary, she dismounted and led the horse.

In 1940, Georgia bought the small cottage Rancho de los Burros, which was on Ghost Ranch property. She began to open it to the world by tearing down walls and replacing them with large panes of glass so that she could see far to the north and west and would have a perfect view of the Pedernal, a flattened mesa that appears in many of her paintings. The house had an inner patio, in which birds, lizards, and snakes made themselves at home.

Georgia spent a great deal of time on the roof of the house. She climbed a wooden ladder to sleep there in her army sleeping bag. She brought friends up to enjoy the stars and moon with her. Her only regret was that the ground at the ranch was not suitable for gardening, and she was forced to travel eighty or more miles to buy supplies and foodstuff.

She had found another property twelve miles south of Ghost Ranch, in the tiny village of Abiquiu. After years of trying to buy it, with its run-down

Black Place #1, 1944. Oil on canvas, 26 x 30⅛". Georgia called this her "favorite place to work" and often made the 150-mile trip to paint the gray hills, which reminded her of "a mile of elephants."
San Francisco Museum of Modern Art, Gift of Charlotte Mack

house, she was at last successful in 1945. She was told that the house sold for two cows, a bushel of corn, and a serape back in 1826, but her purchase price was considerably more. The next three years were spent making it hers, restoring some adobe walls, again replacing others with glass.

At last she had space in which to make the desert bloom. She planted flowers in between rows of corn, rutabagas, endive. She put bright poppies next to the lettuce and made a round onion patch with a rosebush at its center. She grew her own wheat and then ground it for flour to make bread. She planted fruit trees for their blossoms and harvest. Always, she was recreating a sense of her early years on the family's farm.

For company she kept two chow dogs, whose thick furriness made them seem loving when Georgia knew they could be ferocious and unfriendly with strangers. To keep the grasshopper population down in her garden, she raised three turkeys. The turkeys seemed to share her taste in music—they would rest on the windowsill whenever she played her Mantovani records, get up and go as soon as the music stopped.

As she had throughout her life, Georgia continued to greet the dawn with pleasure. Often she would set out on long hikes in the company of her

4

My life is very pleasant this year —

One of the events was a particularly brilliant star where I first came. It was so bright that it made a pattern of star light in my room like pale moonlight — I wonder if you had it in the East. It was so very bright in the evening.

I've been sleeping on the roof this week. I have an army sleeping bag and it is the best out fit I've ever seen for sleeping and. I like to see the sky where I wake and I like the air — and I like rising all over my world with the rising sun.

I have a garden this year. The vegetables

---

chows, carrying a walking stick in case they met snakes along the way. In later years she might rise very early, prepare a cup of tea and sit back to enjoy its warmth while watching her world come to life.

There was never a question in her mind that New Mexico was her spiritual home and had ignited a fresh creative energy in her. According to one young journalist who visited with her in the Southwest, "The Indians say her spirit will walk there when she is gone."

16

Landscapes of the Sky

NOT UNTIL she was in her late sixties did Georgia decide to travel to Europe and other countries around the world. Flying there provided her with a whole new source of ideas to paint. Her tiny sketches of the winding rivers she saw through the airplane window turned into drawings and then grew into large oils that seemed to be intricate and colorful designs.

Inspired by the experience of flying, Georgia began her largest and most ambitious painting when she was seventy-seven. With the help of an assistant, she struggled to prime and stretch rough canvas, twenty-four feet long by eight feet tall. It took repeated attempts to smooth and prepare the heavy canvas with water, glue, and white paint. When it was at last attached to a frame, it completely covered the wall of her double garage at the ranch.

Every morning Georgia mixed pails of paint so that she would have enough of one color to spread across the huge surface. She also had to discover elaborate ways to apply the paint on such a tall, broad surface. To reach the very top of the canvas, she stood on a board suspended between two ten-foot tables. Next, she sat in a chair that she kept moving across the tables. She eventually gave up the chair and stood directly on the tables. By the time she reached the center of the canvas she was able to stand on the floor. She moved into a child's toy Mexican chair to paint the lower sections. At last, she sat right on the floor of the garage, worrying all the time that a rattlesnake might slither in behind her.

Working from early in the morning until late at night, it took her the whole summer of 1965 to complete the work called *Sky Above Clouds, IV*. The finished painting looks serene and mysterious. It gives no hint of the difficulty required to produce it. Hundreds of floating clouds become smooth stepping stones to take us slowly across the sky or inward toward the rosy glow of the horizon. From a distance, the shapes seem to merge into one fluffy white carpet. But truly there is still a border of sky around each cloud through which to peek.

The enormous painting was too large to hang on the wall of one museum and had to be hung on two adjoining walls in another. It is now on loan to the Chicago Art Institute, where it seems to float on a wall that is wide enough to accommodate it. Approaching the shimmering canvas, its eerie glow beckons us to see beyond, to the "wideness and wonder" of O'Keeffe's world.

For her prominent place in the art world, Georgia received numerous awards and honorary degrees from colleges and universities throughout the country. After she was honored by William and Mary, she was to receive similar degrees from the University of Wisconsin, Harvard, Columbia, Brown, and Bryn Mawr. She was elected to the American Academy of Arts, the National Institute of Arts and Letters, and received The Medal of Honor from President Ford in 1977. She received the awards with mixed feelings. At times she mocked them, and at other times, she participated with pride and sincere enjoyment. It almost seemed she was afraid to admit that honors were important to her for fear she would reveal a softness beneath her usually tough exterior.

While Georgia worked as an artist, she tried to insulate herself against the outside world. Yet she could not completely cut out pain and worry caused by wars and economic depression. It led her to experience an emotional depression of her own, which required medical care and prevented her from painting for over a year. After that, she was able to separate herself, somehow, from the troubled concerns of the world in order to concentrate on an ordered world of nature.

Appreciation for her work never faltered after the 1920s, but she had an enthusiastic reception from a new, younger generation following several large retrospective shows in the 1960s and 1970s. Once again her life and personality were of interest along with her art. As each of her shows was arranged, she decided which paintings would be included, made it a point to accompany them to the museum, was adamant about how they would be arranged on the walls and about what color the walls should be. As one museum director said, "Georgia is easy to get along with as long as you do exactly what she wants."

Georgia's sharp eyesight had always been something she took for granted, but with advancing age she found her vision declining. Doctors confirmed that there was nothing they could do to improve her sight. At eighty-four, she was feeling depressed and had almost decided she would have to quit painting when a young man, Juan Hamilton, came to her door offering to help with odd jobs. Georgia checked to find out what Juan's previous life had been and discovered that he had been a potter. She encouraged him to return to his creative work. When Georgia saw the large, smooth pots he created, she knew how talented Juan was and wanted to provide him with the atmosphere of support that Stieglitz had offered early in her career.

She even joined Juan in working with the clay, hoping she might be able to shape beautiful pots for a whole new form of creation.

But she never felt as comfortable handling clay as she did holding her paint brush and, despite her weak eyes, she at last went back to her painting. She found that colors and light looked different to her than before, but with Juan's encouragement she was able to adapt and adjust to her diminished vision.

As she had led Juan back to his clay, he led her back to painting. They became close friends and companions, with Juan gradually taking over much of her business responsibility, as Stieglitz had done earlier. Again there was gossip about their relationship. Georgia had never worried about gossip before. She was certainly not going to let it bother her now.

She and Juan traveled to Washington, D.C., in 1976. They walked from one museum to another, visited all the galleries and the memorials. At the Lincoln Memorial she was deeply moved by the marble monument, but she later insisted to a reporter that she thought "Mr. Lincoln [would not] have been sitting there. He would have been standing." Georgia painted several scenes after their return, calling the series of paintings, *From A Day With Juan.* There is no indication in the strong works that she was not seeing as well as always.

In the summer of 1982, when Georgia was ninety-four, she traveled to an international sculpture show held in San Francisco, to see a piece she had designed on a smaller scale some years earlier. She supervised the casting of the sculpture, which had now grown to eleven feet of painted black aluminum from the original white epoxy piece of a few feet. During the show she posed for photographers in and around the imposing sculpture, while answering questions about art and artists. She was aware that her presence was overshadowing the work of the other sculptors in the show. But she seemed to enjoy the personal attention and found it interesting that this single piece of sculpture should have become a highlight of the exhibition.

The sculpture, called *Abstraction,* is one of her early shapes come to life—almost as a humorous prehistoric creature. Its "head" is turned as if to listen to the comments of the public—something its creator never did. Though through the years much was said about her life and about her paintings, she

Georgia at ninety-four, peering through her sculpture,
Abstraction, 1982.
Vincent Maggiora, Photographer

chose to ignore the comments, using all her energy to produce the very unique art that is O'Keeffe's.

> *I have never cared about what*
> *others were doing in art, or*
> *what they thought of my own*
> *paintings. Why should I care?*
> *I found my inspirations and*
> *painted them.*

Georgia believed in herself and dared to present bold and original subjects in a way they had never before been painted. For over sixty years she continued painting them when others were switching styles to keep up with the latest trends. She once insisted, "I don't think I have a great gift, it isn't just *talent*. You have to have something else. You have to have a kind of nerve. It's mostly a lot of nerve and a lot of very, very hard work."

Early in her career Georgia was called a poet whose symbols seemed to flow without effort onto the canvas. Her words, too, are poetic, especially when she describes what painting has meant to her life:

*One works I suppose because it is the most
interesting thing one knows to do.*

*The days one works are the best days. On the other
days one is hurrying through the other things one
imagines one has to do to keep one's life going.*

*You get the garden planted.
You get the roof fixed.
You take the dog to the vet.
You spend a day with a friend.
You learn to make a new kind of bread.
You hunt up photographs for someone who thinks he
    needs them.
You certainly have to do the shopping.*

*You may even enjoy doing such things.
You think they have to be done. You even think you
have to have some visitors or take a trip to keep
from getting queer living alone with just two chows.
But always you are hurrying through these so that
you can get at the painting again because that is
the high spot—in a way it is what you do all
the other things for.
Why it is that way I do not know.*

*I have no theories to offer.
The painting is like a thread that runs through all
the reasons for all the other things that make one's life.*

THE COLOPHON

Georgia had answered my letter very kindly, explaining she was busy with her own projects and could not help me with mine. As I stood in Abiquiu before the thick pink adobe wall surrounding her home, I wished things were different. I wanted to meet with her, to ask her all my questions, to tell her of my admiration for her life and her work. I stood there longingly for many moments, smelling the pungent lilacs, soaking up the serenity of sky and hills. Then, almost like a mirage, she was in front of me, looking as if she had stepped out of a Stieglitz photograph. Dressed in black, with a jaunty shawl around her shoulders and her narrow-brimmed Gaucho hat firmly on her head, she walked several times around the gravel drive on the arm of a companion. And then she was gone. But not the memory of her. That remains imprinted on my brain. For me, it was a sign that I should go home and complete the book with her inspiration if not her help.

Georgia O'Keeffe died on March 6, 1986, at the age of ninety-eight. Her memory will remain as striking and as vivid as the paintings she has given us.

Georgia and her companion appear for an instant, May 1983.
Charles Gherman, Photographer

NOTES

PAGE

3   *Because time must stop when words are put on paper, birthdays must also come to a halt. It may be most accurate to remember that Georgia was born on November 15, 1887.*

5   "... world for the moment." Mary Braggiotti, "Her Worlds are Many," *New York Post*, May 16, 1946. Quoted in Laurie Lisle, *Portrait of an Artist*, New York: Washington Square Press, 1981, p. 170.

8–9 Details of Georgia's family background are found in Lisle, *Portrait of an Artist*.

10 "If Lake Monona . . . is *that* thunder?" Helen Rank, "Georgia O'Keeffe—Sun Prairie Native," *Sun Prairie Star-Countryman*, September 2, 1948. Quoted in Laurie Lisle, *Portrait of an Artist*, p. 16.

13 "If only people . . . like them better." Francis O'Brien, "Americans We Like: Georgia O'Keeffe," *The Nation*, October 12, 1927, p. 361.

14 The one-room schoolhouse is mentioned in Lisle, *Portrait of an Artist*.

18 "crazy notions." Laurie Lisle, *Portrait of an Artist*, p. 19.

20–21 Reasons for the O'Keeffe move to Williamsburg are found in Lisle, *Portrait of an Artist*.

25 We cannot be certain about the items Francis stocked but these are typical items that would have been found in most stores of those years.

32 "O is for . . . drawings are fine." *Mortar Board Yearbook*, 1905.

36 The Pennsylvania Academy of Fine Arts was criticized for its unique attempt to include women in life

drawing classes.
Charlotte Streifer Rubinstein, *American Women Artists,* New York: Avon Books, 1982, p. 92.

37   Details about Aunt Ollie's work are found in Lisle, *Portrait of an Artist.*

49   "didn't look . . . about drawing." Dorothy Norman, *Alfred Stieglitz: An American Seer.* New York: Viking Press, 1963, p. 11.

50   "likely to go . . . most appalling." J.E. Chamberlain, *Camera Work,* No. 23, July 1908, pp. 10–11. Quoted in Dorothy Norman, *Alfred Stieglitz: An American Seer.*

53   "What I knew . . . to the moon," Perry Miller Adato, *Georgia O'Keeffe,* Film, 1977.

55   "Fill a space . . . beautiful way." Ibid.

57   "I wouldn't . . . wasn't for him." Letter from O'Keeffe to Anita Pollitzer, August 25, 1915. Collection of American Literature, The Beinecke Rare Book and Manuscript Library, Yale University.

58   "modern art to . . . American public." Robert Myron and Sundell, *Modern Art in America.* New York: Crowell-Collier Press, 1971, p. 69.

59   "was different . . . without much else." Anita Pollitzer, "That's Georgia," *Saturday Review of Literature,* November 4, 1950, p. 51.

63   Details of Georgia's relationship with Arthur Macmahon are found in Lisle, *Portrait of an Artist.*

65   "I wonder . . . these things," Letter from O'Keeffe to Anita Pollitzer, December 13, 1915. Collection of American Literature, The Beinecke

Rare Book and Manuscript Library, Yale University.

66 "Anita—do you . . . I know of." Ibid. October 11, 1915.

57 "Finally, a woman . . . a long while." Anita Pollitzer, *Saturday Review of Literature*, p. 41.

Some feel Stieglitz did not really use the words, "Finally, woman on paper," but we can be sure he was impressed by what he saw. We also know he had encouraged women artists and shown their work in his gallery.

68 "said something" Letter from O'Keeffe to Anita Pollitzer, January 4, 1916, The Beinecke Library.

68 "Words and I . . . friends at all." Alexander Eliot, *Three Hundred Years of American Painters*, New York: Time, 1957.

69 ". . . it makes me . . . a fool's game." Letter from O'Keeffe to Anita Pollitzer, January 4, 1916. The Beinecke Library.

71 ". . . they're really . . . own affairs." Grace Glueck, "It's Just What's In My Head," *New York Times*, Sunday, October 18, 1970.

71–72 "They have . . . terribly thirsty." Letter from O'Keeffe to Anita Pollitzer, November 27, 1916, The Beinecke Library.

74 "The whole sky . . . hotness of it—" Ibid. September 16, 1916.

74 "through the thickness . . . as well . . ." Letter from O'Keeffe to Anita Pollitzer, February 4, 1916, The Beinecke Library.

74–76   Reactions of Canyon friends to Georgia's art are found in Lisle, *Portrait of an Artist.*

76   "watermelon" Response by a friend who taught with Georgia, from Laurie Lisle, *Portrait of an Artist,* p. 104

76   "strange art" Henry Tyrrell, "Esoteric Art at '291' " *Christian Science Monitor,* May 4, 1917.

78   "In three minutes . . . you could imagine." Perry Miller Adato, *Georgia O'Keeffe,* Film.

78   "The tall tripod . . . my reprieve." Sue Davidson Lowe, *Stieglitz: A Memoir/Biography,* New York: Farrar, Straus, Giroux, 1983, p. 180.

78   "composite portrait" *Alfred Stieglitz, Catalogue of Exhibit,* National Gallery of Art, Washington, D.C., 1983.

80   "racing man . . . for a winner." Mahonri Sharp Young, *Painters of the Stieglitz Group: Early American Moderns,* New York: Watson-Guptill Publishers, 1974.

84   "three loving eyes . . . his camera." Sue Davidson Lowe, *Stieglitz: A Memoir/Biography,* p. 223.

87–88   "I do want . . . real homes." Letter from Alfred Stieglitz to Mrs. Alfred S. Rossin (Clara) February 2, 1927. The Beinecke Library.

88   "tried to keep . . . word was 'no.' " Perry Miller Adato, *Georgia O'Keeffe,* Film.

90   "America seems . . . and novelists." Edmund Wilson, *New Republic,* March 18, 1925, p. 97.

90   "very annoyed . . . artist," Mary Lynn Kotz, "A Day with Georgia O'Keeffe," *Art News,* December, 1977.

90 "Georgia outblazes . . . other painters . . ." Edmund Wilson, *New Republic*.

90 "freak" Statement by sculptor Louise Nevelson, in Laurie Lisle, *Portrait of an Artist*, p. 53.

90 "all the male . . . stop painting." Grace Glueck, *New York Times*.

91 "this girl . . . and failing." Dorothy Norman. *Alfred Stieglitz: An American Seer*, p. 131.

91 "for a woman . . . work of a man." Sue Davidson Lowe, *Stieglitz: A Memoir/Biography*, p. 258.

91 "dirty colors" Perry Miller Adato, *Georgia O'Keeffe*, Film.

91 Stieglitz's divorce from his first wife was final in September, 1924.

93 "I've had . . . my own." Carol Taylor, "Lady Dynamo," *New York World Telegram*, March 31, 1945. Quoted in Laurie Lisle, *Portrait of an Artist*, p. 160.

93 "Why don't . . . your face?" Ibid, p. 360.

93 "The meaning . . . I painted." *Examiner*, New York, October 25, 1970, unnamed author.

93 "Making a decision . . . other things." Mary Lynn Kotz, *Art News*.

94 "on call . . . twenty people." Herbert Seligmann, *America and Alfred Stieglitz A Collective Portrait*, Edited by Waldo Frank, et al., New York: Literary Guild, 1934, p. 113.

96 "everything close . . . in layers." Beth Coffelt, "A Visit with Georgia O'Keeffe," California Living, *San Francisco Sunday Examiner and Chronicle*, April 11, 1971.

101 "Sometimes . . . in sight." Leo Janos, "O'Keeffe at Eighty-four." *Atlantic Monthly*, December, 1971.

101 "That's my backyard," Alfred Frankenstein, "No Ordinary Autobiography," *San Francisco Chronicle*, March 15, 1971, p. 37.

107 "The Indians . . . she is gone." Beth Coffelt, *San Francisco Sunday Examiner and Chronicle*.

110 "wideness and wonder" Lloyd Goodrich and Doris Bry, *Georgia O'Keeffe*. Exhibition and Catalogue, Whitney Museum of Art, 1970–1971, p. 25.

111 "Georgia is . . . she wants." Douglas Davis, "O'Keeffe Country," *Newsweek*, November 22, 1976.

113 "Mr. Lincoln . . . standing." Mary Lynn Kotz, *Art News*.

113 Georgia created the original sculpture in 1945.

115 "I have never . . . painted them." Leo Janos, *Atlantic Monthly*.

115 "I don't think . . . very hard work." Mary Lynn Kotz, *Art News*.

116 "One works . . . one's life." Lee Nordness, Editor, *Art: USA: Now*, New York: Viking Press, 1963, pp. 35–36.

BIBLIOGRAPHY

Adato, Perry Miller. *Georgia O'Keeffe*. Film, WNET, New York Films Incorporated. National Endowment, 1977. (Part of a series, "The Originals/Women in Art.")

Carroll, Jon. "Georgia O'Keeffe, Grand Old Lady of Art.'" *San Francisco Chronicle*, August 24, 1982.

Coffelt, Beth. "A Visit with Georgia O'Keeffe." California Living, *San Francisco Sunday Examiner and Chronicle*, April, 11, 1971.

Davis, Douglas. "O'Keeffe Country." *Newsweek*, November 22, 1976.

Duthy, Robin. "Unlimited Editions." *Connoisseur*, August, 1984.

Eliot, Alexander. *Three Hundred Years of American Painters*. New York: Time, 1957.

Frank, Waldo, Lewis Mumford, Dorothy Norman, Paul Rosenfeld, Harold Rugg, editors. *America and Alfred Stieglitz: A Collective Portrait*. New York: Doubleday, 1934.

Frankenstein, Alfred. "No Ordinary Autobiography." *San Francisco Chronicle*, March 15, 1971, page 37.

Glueck, Grace. "It's Just What's In My Head." *New York Times*, Sunday, October 18, 1970.

Goodrich, Lloyd and Doris Bry. *Georgia O'Keeffe*. Exhibition and Catalogue, Whitney Museum of Art, 1970–1971.

Goossen, E. C. "O'Keeffe." *Vogue Magazine*, March, 1967.

Henkes, Robert. *Eight American Women Painters*. New York: Gordon Press, 1977.

Hoffman, Katherine. *An Enduring Spirit: The Art of Georgia O'Keeffe*. New Jersey: The Scarecrow Press, Inc., 1984.

Homer, William Innes. *Alfred Stieglitz and the American Avant-Garde.* Boston: New York Graphic Society, 1977.

Howard, Maureen, "Forbidden Fruits." *Vogue Magazine,* March, 1982.

Hurt, Frances Hallam. "Famed Artist Georgia O'Keeffe Still Has Ties with Virginia." *Richmond Times Dispatch,* Sunday, April 16, 1978.

Israel, Franklin. "Architectural Digest Visits: Georgia O'Keeffe." *Architectural Digest,* July, 1981.

Janos, Leo. "O'Keeffe at Eighty-four." *Atlantic Monthly,* December, 1971.

Kotz, Mary Lynn. "A Day with Georgia O'Keeffe." *Art News,* December, 1977.

Kramer, Hilton. "Georgia O'Keeffe." Book Review, *New York Times,* December 12, 1976.

Kuh, Katherine. *The Artist's Voice: Talks with Seventeen Artists.* New York: Harper & Row, 1962.

Lisle, Laurie. *Portrait of an Artist: A Biography of Georgia O'Keeffe.* New York: Washington Square Press, 1980.

Looney, Ralph. "Georgia O'Keeffe." *The Atlantic Monthly,* April, 1965.

Lowe, Sue Davidson, *Stieglitz: A Memoir/Biography.* New York: Farrar, Straus Giroux, 1983.

McBride, Henry. "Curious Responses to Work of Miss Georgia O'Keeffe on Others." *New York Herald,* February 4, 1923.

Messinger, Lisa Mintz. *Georgia O'Keeffe.* Fall Bulletin, The Metropolitan Museum of Art, 1984.

The Mortar Board. Yearbook. Chatham Episcopal Institute, Chatham, Virginia, 1905.

Munro, Eleanor. *Originals: American Women Artists.* New York: Touchstone Books, Simon and Schuster, 1982.

Myron, Robert and Abner Sundell. *Modern Art in America.* New York: Crowell-Collier Press, 1971.

National Gallery of Art. *Alfred Stieglitz.* Catalogue of Exhibit, Washington, D.C., 1983.

Newhall, Beaumont. *The History of Photography.* New York: Museum of Modern Art, 1981.

Nordness, Lee, editor. *Art: USA: Now.* New York: Viking Press, 1963.

Norman, Dorothy. *Alfred Stieglitz: An American Seer.* New York: Random House, 1973.

O'Brien, Frances. "Americans We Like: Georgia O'Keeffe." *The Nation,* October 12, 1927.

O'Keeffe, Georgia. *About Painting Desert Bones. Georgia O'Keeffe: Paintings—1943.* Exhibition Catalogue, An American Place, 1944.

_____. *Georgia O'Keeffe.* New York: Viking Press, 1976.

_____. *Some Memories of Drawings: Georgia O'Keeffe.* New York: Atlantis Editions, 1974.

Pollitzer, Anita. "That's Georgia." *Saturday Review of Literature,* November 4, 1950.

Rubinstein, Charlotte Streifer. *American Women Artists.* New York: Avon Books, 1982.

Seiberling, Dorothy. "Horizons of a Pioneer." *Life Magazine,* March 1, 1968.

Seligmann, Herbert J. "291: A Vision Through Photography," *America and Alfred Stieglitz A Collective Portrait,* Edited by Waldo Frank, et al. New York: Literary Guild, 1934.

Tompkins, Calvin. "Georgia O'Keeffe—The Rose in the Eye Looked Pretty Fine." *New Yorker,* March 4, 1974.

Trenton, Pat. *Picturesque Images From Taos and Santa Fe.* Exhibition Catalogue, January 12–March 17, 1974.

Tyrrell, Henry. "Esoteric Art at '291.'" *Christian Science Monitor.* May 4, 1917.

Wilson, Edmund. "Stieglitz Exhibition at Anderson Galleries." *New Republic,* March 18, 1925.

Young, Mahonri Sharp. *Painters of the Stieglitz Group: Early American Moderns.* New York: Watson–Guptill Publishers, 1974.

INDEX